101 Grassroots Marketing Tips and Tricks

by

Rebecca Davis
"The Medicare Wonder Woman"

Copyright

Copyright 2021. All rights reserved. No part of this book may be reproduced, stored in a retrieval system, or transmitted in any form or by any means: electronic, mechanical, photocopy, recording, scanning, or other means in any manner without the express written consent of the author.

Published in Winter Haven, FL. by Horton International Ministries, Inc.
Editor: RAS Editing,
RASFinalEdit@gmail.com

All inquiries should be sent to:
Kannonball Insurance Solutions, LLC
2104 W Washington Street
Stephenville, TX 76401 or
info@kbisolutionsllc.com

This book may be purchased in bulk orders for educational, training or sales promotions.
Print 1 – July, 2021

Rebecca Davis

Acknowledgements

I would like to thank those that have encouraged, contributed, and helped me along the way.

First and foremost, I am grateful for my clients and all the wonderful people I have met along the way!! I could not do this or be where I am today if it were not for each of you.

This is a list of my favorite podcasters:

Faye Saxon Horton - "I Sell Medicare Plans"
Victoria Cabrera - "The Medicare Space"
Christian Brindle - "Taco Tuesday"
Teresa Kitchens - "Power Woman In Insurance"
Allie Saleh – "Strong LYFE Podcast"

A Special thank you to the following contributors:
Lavet Ranae Ferchert
Hermila Perreault
Faye Saxon Horton
The entire Kannonball Insurance Team

I owe many thanks for my fantastic book cover created by Secure Agent Marketing with photos by Allison Ballinger.

A special note of gratitude to the following family members:

To my faithful husband, Jeremy, who has stood by me during my constant phone conversations about insurance, business trips, working late nights, and all my crazy ideas, words cannot express how lucky I am to have you by my side.

Rebecca Davis

To my beautiful Maci who has been a trooper helping your dad at events and always willing to lend a helping hand. We could not have done this without your help.

To my brother, Ron, who has always been there through thick and thin. You picked me up when I fell and dusted me off; you are loved more than you know.

To my Assistant, Melisa, who does her very best to keep me focused and organized every day, thank you. You are family in every sense of the word!

To my mom who is looking down upon me from above, you were always my greatest cheerleader and supporter. Without you I would not be the woman I am today!

To my dad who has always pushed me to be better, to be true to my word and to be "honest as the day is long." Thank you both for being amazing parents.

Now, Kannon, you are the center of my world. You, little boy, are my inspiration to it all. My life changed forever the minute you entered it. Every day you bring new light into my life. You made me a mom and inspired me to be a business owner and now a writer. It is because of you I can help others aspire to live their dreams with epic success!

I'm constantly striving to make all of you proud of me every day.

Thank you so very much! Rebecca

Rebecca Davis

Contents

Copyright 2
Acknowledgements 3
Introduction 12
COMPLIANCE 17
#1 – Marketing Box 18
#2 – Donut Day 19
#3 – Social Media 20
#4 – Fourth of July 21
#5 – The Phone 22
#6 – Sports Team 23
#7 – Cheering Squad 24
#8 – Card Game Tournament 25
#9 – Lead Stand 26
#10 – Lunch and Learn 27
#11 – Pharmacy Jars 28
#12 – Speaking Engagements 29
#13 – Family 4th Event 30
#14 – Old School 31
#15 – Coffee for Everyone 32
#16 – National Holiday 33
#17 – Cooking Class 34
#18 – Happy Birthday 35
#19 - Newsletter 36
#20 – Low Income Subsidy (LIS) Party 38

#21 - Your Book..39

#22 – Chamber of Commerce 40

#23 – Angel Tree 42

#24 – BNI Group...43

#25 - Funerals 44

#26 – Senior Center Workouts.......................................45

#27 - Kindness..46

#28 – The Flea Market 47

#29 – Leads at Breakfast 48

#30 – B I N G O!..49

#31 – Provider Marketing 50

#32 – Meals on Wheels 51

#33 – Attend Church...52

#34 – Local Services 53

#35 – Golf Tournament...55

#36 – Medicare Carwash 56

#37 – Walking Group 57

#38 - YouTube 58

#39 – Movie Night 59

#40 – Podcast...60

#41 – Hand Sanitizers 61

#42 – Partner with P&C Agents 62

#43 – Food Drive 63

#44 – Paint Party..64

Rebecca Davis

#45 – Custom Music 65

#46 – Taxi Billboards 66

#47 – Game Night 67

#48 – Air Fresheners 68

#49 – Movie Night 69

#50 – Tik Tok 70

#51 – Educating the Incarcerated 71

#52 – Local Grocers 72

#53 – Walmart Pharmacy 73

#54 – A Blog 74

#55 – Customized Golf Balls 75

#56 – Easter Egg Hunt 76

#57 – Garage Sale 77

#58 – Corn Hole Tournament 78

#59 – Valentine Brunch 79

#60 – Ice Cream Social 80

#61 – Turkey Giveaway 81

#62 - Tech Classes 82

#63 – Couponing 83

#64 – Everyone in the Pool 84

#65 – Grandparents Day 85

#66 – Casino Night 86

#67 – Help in HR 87

#68 – Senior Iron Man 88

#69 – Christmas Carols 89

#70 – Grow an Herb Garden 90

#71 – Financial Advisors 91

#72 – Disability Attorneys 92

#73 – Help Veterans 93

#74 – Christmas Festival 94

#75 - Tailgate Party 96

#76 – Insurance Agents 97

#77 – Social Influencers 98

#78 – Pie Baking Contest 99

#79 – Singles Senior Group 100

#80 – Senior Safety Class 101

#81 – Needle Point Group 102

#82 – Medicare Survival Kit 103

#83 - Free Leads 104

#84 –Senior Haircut Day 105

#85 – Medicare Jeopardy 106

#86 – Senior Calendar 107

#87 – Health Fair 108

#88 – The Mutt Strut 109

#89 – Yard Signs 112

#90 – Table Tents 113

#91 – Billboards 114

#92 – Kentucky Derby Party 115

Rebecca Davis

#93 – Outdoor Movie Night 116
#94 – Dance, Dance, Dance 117
#95 – Bus trip 118
#96 – Senior Clothes Closet 119
#97 – A Grief Group 120
#98 – The Senior Choir 121
#99 – Special Occasion 122
#100 – B.I.N.G.O 123
#101 – Cool Stuff 124
BONUS TIP 125
   Remind Magazine 125
Appendix 127
Where to Find Rebecca Davis 130

Introduction

Hi, I am Rebecca Davis, the "Medicare Wonder Woman," because I take the wonder out of Medicare.

I originally got my start in the insurance industry as a captive agent with *State Farm* back in 2012. I am amazed how much success a person can have in the insurance business, yet nobody ever tells you about it when you're young (that is unless your parents happen to already be in this business.)

You never see insurance as a career at a high school or college job fair and you should! Insurance always seems like something a person stumbles across or falls into. For me, I fell into the business.

Before I started at *State Farm* I managed a chain of retail stores, while being pregnant. I remember being at work on the retail floor, helping a client. Suddenly, I felt a gush

Rebecca Davis

and immediately excused myself to discover that I was hemorrhaging.

I was rushed to the hospital where I stayed a couple of days, after which my Mom picked me up and took me home. I wasn't at home for more than a couple of hours and it happened again. This time the hemorrhaging was worse than the first time. Thank goodness my Mom was still there and rushed me back to the hospital.

Once there they checked the baby and the next thing I knew I was being prepped for emergency surgery. My son was trying to come but with nowhere to go. Even though my body just wasn't ready, he was ready to be born a month early.

Within the next 30 minutes he was delivered via emergency C-Section and I got to see him for the first time. The instant I saw him, I knew I did not want to work retail stores ever again. I didn't want to work nights. I didn't want to work weekends. I didn't want to work on holidays. My entire world just changed at that moment, yet I had no idea how much it truly was about to change.

Once released from the hospital, my son and I went home on leave to heal and be together. While I had the time, I started combing the help wanted ads and lived on the *Indeed* website.

This is when I found *State Farm*. Workdays were Monday through Friday, 9 to 5, with weekends and holidays off, and, they were going to pay me to sell something that people legally should have.

My first thought was, how hard can that be? (LOL) Little did I know it was harder than you would think? Anyways, I thought it was perfect. I applied, got the job pending getting licensed. I got Life, Health, Property & Casualty licenses in the next two weeks. The day the doctor released me I was ready to go to work.

Rebecca Davis

I worked for *State Farm* the next four years but realized I wasn't going anywhere. I wanted more. I did some research and decided I needed to be independent and sell Medicare.

In 2016 I went through my first Medicare Annual Enrollment Period (AEP). In 2017 my agency, *Kannonball Insurance Solutions, LLC* opened its doors. The agency was named after my son, Kannon (with a K) since he was the whole reason I fell into the insurance space.

During that time, my husband was deployed on a Navy ship. We only got to communicate about once a month over the phone and letters here and there. Everything he earned went towards bills. We had no extra money to grow my new business. So, I had to be creative.

I had to figure out how to get leads without buying leads. I had to figure out how to leverage the carriers into helping me. But, I was just getting started nobody knew who I was yet. I had to figure out how to make a name for myself.

So, what did I do? I invested in my community and into my business with good "ole-fashioned" sweat equity that I call "Grassroots Marketing." Over the next several pages I am going to give you all the things I have done to get my business where it is today.

I, personally, never bought a lead during the first three years in business and created a highly successful agency just by doing Grassroots Marketing.

Rebecca Davis

COMPLIANCE

Remember, before you decide on any event, to check with the Center for Medicare and Medicaid Services (CMS) and the insurance carrier, if you plan to represent one, on the compliance rules and regulations.

Depending on the style of the event you choose, the rules can vary. So make sure you have everything in proper order when you are doing events.

Always be aware of the compliance rules, so you can help as many people as possible all while protecting them and you!

#1 – Marketing Box

Always keep a marketing box in your car.

What is a marketing box, you ask?

A marketing box contains Business Cards, Flyers, tape, thumbtacks, mini stapler, personalized pens, carrier giveaways, Business Reply Cards (BRC), cheap gift cards, hand sanitizer, masks, handi-wipes. You never know when an opportunity may arise!

Pro Tip: Customize everything you can with your information and branding.

Rebecca Davis

#2 – Donut Day

Celebrate National Donut Day.

In honor of National Donut Day, pick up several small boxes of donuts and drop them off at all your favorite provider's offices, including hearing, vision, dental offices, Medicaid and Social Security offices. Leave donuts at any place where you could potentially get a referral or have gotten a referral.

Pro tip: Walk in the door saying. "Happy National Donut Day from (Your name or your branding)."

#3 – Social Media

Be involved in your local Facebook groups.

The "Buy-Sell" and the "Rant and Rave" pages work well. When people look for a specific service and you know a guy or a business tag and promote them. They will in turn do the same for you and maybe even use your services.

Pro tip: Tag current business clients first. Your clients will continue to make money and continue to pay their bills. This will also ensure that they will become big promoters of you and your business!

#4 – Fourth of July

Join the Independence Day (July 4th) parade.

Does your town do a 4th of July parade?

If so, sign-up, make a float and be a part of the community!! Toss out candy and other small items with your name and contact information. We usually do those rubber bracelets with our name and number on them. T-shirts are great too!

Pro tip: Invite your clients to ride on the float or in the car with you, they will have a blast! Note: Secure waivers.

#5 – The Phone

Answer your dang phone!!
(Personal pet peeve of mine)

None of this does any good if you don't answer your phone when a prospective client calls. Make sure you check your messages and return calls promptly.

Also, make sure the voicemail message makes sense and relates to what you are selling. Do not just use the standard greeting; actually, record a professional voicemail greeting!

Pro Tip: It's not hard to be successful in this business. You start by always answering your phone.

Rebecca Davis

#6 – Sports Team

Sponsor a Pickleball team.

Sponsor the local seniors Pickleball team. Ask at local gyms and street lot play areas if there are any senior Pickleball teams.

If no teams are available, form a team. Bring seniors out to play together and mingle. Provide T- shirts with logos. You might form teams from various communities and conduct a series of competitions.

Pro Tip: Show up at the games and cheer your team on. Bring snacks and water bottles with your label on them. Pass water out to the spectators as well as the team.

#7 – Cheering Squad

Sponsor a Senior Cheering Squad.

All grandparents want to see their grandchildren play sports. Coordinate a cheering section for a team made up of grandparents.

Provide banners and signs for the grandparents to cheer their teams on.

Pro Tip: Spectators will know the team has a cheering squad sponsored by your agency. Bring snacks and water, personalized with your label, to pass out to the team and the grandparents.

Rebecca Davis

#8 – Card Game Tournament

Hold a Card Game Tournament.

Host a Bridge or Hearts Tournament at the local library or community center. Seniors love to play cards. Each playing table can be sponsored by a different carrier and include snacks.

Pro Tip: Crown the Game Champions. Bring prizes to each game day. Give larger prizes for the champions. All prizes should be branded with your information.

#9 – Lead Stand

Order a Lead Stand from one of the prominent carriers in your market.

A Lead Stand is used as a kiosk to gather permission to call slips. Put the stand in restaurants, salons, libraries, or wherever you have made friends in the community.

Every few days, go by and check for leads. Check the business where the stand is located. See if there is anything you can help them with.

Pro Tip: Get several and put them in multiple locations.

Rebecca Davis

#10 – Lunch and Learn

Conduct a lunch and learn with all the local Realtors.

Explain to the Realtors how moving in and out of town, or in and out of the state, could affect their client's insurance. Generally, Medicare and Individual Health Beneficiaries have two months to make changes. This could be different depending on when notifications of a move are made to Social Security and/or the insurance company.

Let the Realtors know, depending on the type of insurance, missing the opportunity to change could potentially cause the client to lose coverage.

Pro Tip: Offer joint marketing strategies from which you both can benefit.

#11 – Pharmacy Jars

Leave Candy Jars at the local Pharmacies.

Introduce yourself and let the pharmacy manager know what you do and how you might be able to help with a claim issue. Go back every couple of weeks to say "Hi," refill their jar and drop off more business cards!

Pro tip- Some carriers have containers that make the cutest little candy jars!

Rebecca Davis

#12 – Speaking Engagements

<u>Volunteer speaking engagements at the local High School or Colleges</u>.

Offer to conduct a life skills lecture about how insurance works. Explain the different types of insurance and cover the components of insurance, e.i. deductible, copay, coinsurance and maximums.

Let the audience know that when they finish school, being an insurance professional is a great career opportunity.

Pro Tip: Take T-shirts with your business logo to give out. Students will wear them, especially if they are cool!

#13 – Family 4th Event

Host a family friendly 4th of July Event.

We did a meet and greet with the Paw Patrol. We gave soda floats and temporary tattoos of our company log on everyone who volunteered.

Then, all the participants went to the city sponsored festivities with my logo on their arms and faces. There was a line of people wrapped around our building for this event. Get an insurance carrier involved to help pay for it all!

Pro Tip: Make a Facebook event page for it and invite the whole town!

Rebecca Davis

#14 – Old School

Let's go old school...

Post flyers about your business or your upcoming event on every available board in town. Leave the flyers at restaurants, farm stores, churches, pawn shops, laundromats, grocers, dry cleaners, hair salons, barbershops, watch repair shops, realtors, spas and health clubs, carwash, bookstores… get it in any and every place that comes to mind. *NO PLACE IS OFF LIMITS!*

Pro Tip: Use different flyers at different locations or different type locations so that you know which ones are working.

#15 – Coffee for Everyone

Buy Coffee for Everyone!

Now and then I will swing through one of my favorite coffee drive-through spots on a Friday and hand the cashier my credit card or a few hundred dollars.

I will ask the attendant to pay for each person's coffee in line behind me until the money runs out. In return, I only ask that they give the person my business card and say, "...it's give back Friday from *Kannonball Insurance*."

Pro Tip: Buy the checkout person a cup of coffee or leave a noticeable tip. Switch spots so you give back to different people. This works great in the summer with snow cones.

Rebecca Davis

#16 – National Holiday

Celebrate a National Holiday

Each day and each month of the year is designated as some national holiday. Choose a day that fits the environment in your area. Celebrate the day by advertising giveaways or something as simple as coffee and Danish at your office. Example: National House Plant Day. Give small potted plants as giveaways to people who attend. Play music. Prepare cards about growing house plants.

Pro Tip: This could be any day that best fits what you are able to put the energy and time into making a fun event. Bottom line you will get free leads.

#17 – Cooking Class

Host a cooking class in your office for people with chronic illnesses.

Invite nutritionists or chefs in or make it yourself. Host a cooking class that teaches the best practices for eating healthy and keeping diabetes or health disease in check.

Do a live demonstration in which the guests can participate and when the food is ready, sit around a table together and try it. Don't forget to give away door prizes.

Pro Tip: Invite current chronic plan members and tell them to bring a friend. Also *Pampered Chef*™ associates are great to host it!

Rebecca Davis

#18 – Happy Birthday

The Birthday Call...

Send birthday cards monthly, but also do a telephone call on the actual day of the client's birthday. On the call sing the Happy Birthday song. Yes, it is sometimes awkward but get over it because they love it. If there's no answer, sing it into voicemail.

Pro Tip: Treat this as a singing telegram. The minute they answer the phone, go right into "Happy Birthday." At the end, tell the birthday guest who you are. Most of my clients can actually figure out that it's me.

#19 - Newsletter

The Newsletter...

If you are not doing this yet, I highly encourage you to do so. This is a great way to stay in contact with your people on a personal level. I've seen several different styles. There is no wrong way to do a newsletter (except, perhaps not doing a newsletter at all).

My newsletter is in letter format and I personally write it. I like the letter versus a newspaper look with columns because I feel it comes across more personal.

The Newsletter is issued quarterly to give enough time to have different things to say so the Newsletter doesn't become boring.

Many clients thank us for the Newsletter. Clients love the fact that we stay in touch throughout the year.

Rebecca Davis

Each Newsletter has three parts or more:

1. Introduction – the Introduction acknowledges what's going on and expresses what we have been doing lately.

2. A Newsletter should let the reader know what is new with your business of importance to them, like plan changes, etc.

3. The Newsletter should always include all the different ways to reach you.

You can always add more or change this up. <u>A sample of our Newsletter is in the Appendix.</u>

Pro Tip: Address by handwriting and use colored envelopes so they stand out in the mail.

Low Income Subsidy (LIS) Party

u want to get more LIS people coming to you? Then, have an LIS party!

You can do this at your office, a library or any place that has private space. This is a great way to get potential low income clients in your door. Help them do the application for LIS and once approved enroll them in a plan.

Some carriers have specific flyers which they will customize and mail for your event. I recommend having a LIS party the same day every month.

Pro Tip: There are some different compliance rules with this marketing. Make sure you understand the marketing guidelines before doing the event.

Rebecca Davis

#21 - Your Book

<u>Write a book.</u>

Distinguish yourself by being a master at your craft. It will create a celebrity-like following and give you something to talk about initially with a new client.

Writing a book is not nearly as complicated as it sounds. Don't be afraid to do it. Even I did it!

Pro Tip: Use your book as a giveaway for senior events.

#22 – Chamber of Commerce

Join the local Chamber of Commerce and get involved in the events they sponsor.

Did you know as a member of your local Chamber of Commerce you have access to the member's list?

Get the list of local businesses. Write a letter that introduces you and the services/products you offer and how you would love to help other members. Then mail the letters off!

Your local Chamber is also responsible for many events within your community. Make sure you become a part these events by setting up a table or being a sponsor. Support your community and they will support you.

Be proactive in contacting and networking with other Chamber members by attending new business grand openings and chamber mixers. Refer to their businesses and ask them to refer to your business.

Rebecca Davis

Pro Tip: Be sure to add your *FaceBook™* information to the letter. Anyone who likes your page will enter a drawing for a prize!

#23 – Angel Tree

Host the Angel Tree at your Office.

Volunteer to host the Angel Tree at your office. This is a great cause and it gets people coming to your door that may not normally come in.

This is a seasonal project, however it is one in which the community will generally participate. Check with your local Child Protective Services (CPS) and Senior centers for angels and ask them to advertise that you have their angels available at your business.

Pro Tip: Do both a children's Angel Tree and a Senior Angel Tree.

Rebecca Davis

#24 – BNI Group

Join a BNI Group...

Business Network International (BNI) is a franchised networking group where trusting and reciprocal relationships are built.

Generally, there is one representative of each various business group, i.e. insurance, accounting, plumbers, attorneys, etc. Each member of the group contributes to the success of each other's members through inner-group referrals.

Pro Tip: Many insurance agents in these groups say 20% of their business comes from the group.

#25 - Funerals

Attend a client's funeral.

When you learn of the death of a client, and time permits, show support to the family by attending the viewing or funeral. Introduce yourself and let the family know that you enjoyed your time with their loved one.

Family and friends will naturally ask you how you knew the deceased. Let them know you were the Medicare and/or Life Insurance agent. Often your clients will talk about you to their families. Leave your card in case the family needs any assistance.

Pro Tip: Volunteer to help sort out any final medical bills or any other issues that you are able to help solve.

Rebecca Davis

#26 – Senior Center Workouts

Host a Senior Friendly exercise class!

Visit the local senior centers in your area and ask if they are doing exercise classes. Let them know that this is an activity that you would be interested in helping them out with. Active seniors equal healthier seniors, and healthier seniors live longer happier lives.

Pro Tip: Remember to have all exercises chair friendly; not all seniors are very mobile.

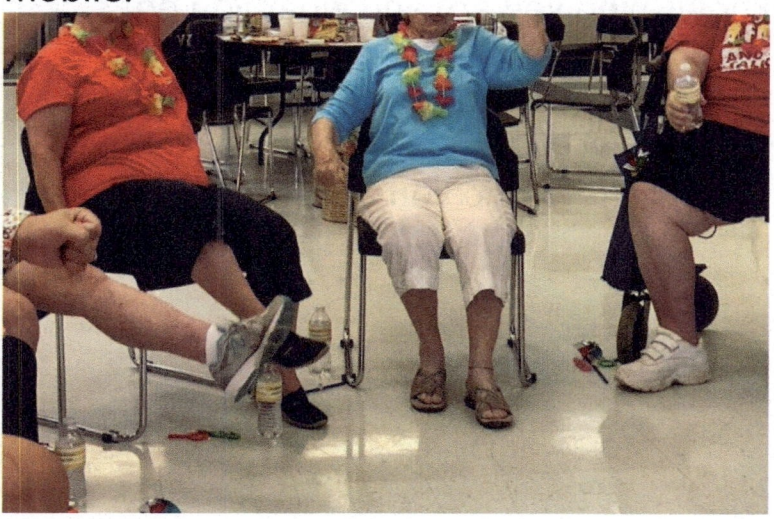

#27 - Kindness

Random Acts of Kindness!

This works best if you have a walk-in office location. Post a giveaway on *Facebook*, get them to like and share your page and then draw a name from the group. The winner must come to the office to pick up the gift.

When they come into the office to claim their prize, it gives you the chance to let them know who you are and what your business is all about. They may or may not need your services, but, someone else now knows who you are and what you do.

Pro Tip: Take a picture with the winner, post on *Facebook*, and tag them so their friends know who you are as well.

Rebecca Davis

#28 – The Flea Market

Set up a booth at the local Flea Market.

Seniors love Flea Markets. They love the buy/sell/trade spaces as they live for a great treasure hunt. You will find a lot of your target market at these locations.

Pro Tip: Use a spinning wheel for free stuff or conduct a drawing for a basket. This is a great way to get them to stop and approach you or ask what you are giving away.
Remember: Keep the gifts under $15 per person.

#29 – Leads at Breakfast

Need some free leads? Eat at the same breakfast spot everyday between 6:15 a.m. and 7:30 a.m. That's the sweet spot!

Bring your work stuff and make friends with the local people, as well as the staff. Ask questions about known roads in the area and say, "Thanks, I've got someone to help out that way today."

Eventually, usually about a week to a month, you will find that everyone will know who you are and what you do. People will start to bring their policies for review over a cup of coffee.

Pro Tip: Wear your "Ask Me About Medicare" button and your silver sneakers.

Rebecca Davis

#30 – B I N G O!

Seniors Love Bingo!

Hit up your local library and get on their calendar to do an informal sales Bingo event every month on the same day. This way it becomes routine, and the seniors will not get confused on what day you are doing Bingo.

Dollar store items are great for prizes. We use *Lysol* wipes, shampoo, conditioner, candles, toilet paper, crossword puzzle books, etc. Seniors actually love this stuff because they need it and it saves money out of their budget.

Pro Tip: Each month pick a different carrier to feature and ask each carrier to do a mailing for your event to drive seniors there.

#31 – Provider Marketing

Visit with the Providers….

If I've said it once, I've said it a thousand times. I cannot stress enough that you must visit local doctors, dentists, chiropractors, vision doctors, mental health doctors, urgent care providers, etc.

Talk to them, befriend them. Let them know if they have a billing or claims issue you can help. Let them know you are an expert with all the plans you represent and can make sure their patients are taken care of properly.

Let the dental and vision providers know about plans that can get the low-income patients in their door to be treated.

Pro Tip: Bring a basket of goodies to give with a stack of business cards to put on display.

Rebecca Davis

#32 – Meals on Wheels

Volunteer to help deliver meals and meet the seniors in person.

Visit the local *Meals on Wheels* chapter and find out what they are all about; how they get donations and share with them what you do and how you can help the low-income seniors in the area.

Pro Tip: Bonus points for hosting an event that can bring seniors and donations together on behalf of the Chapter.

#33 – Attend Church

Do you attend Church?

If so, then get involved with church activities. Reach out to your pastor or priest and ask if you can host a monthly senior mixer and each month a different activity. Generally, they are thrilled with this idea.

Pro tip- Wear the "Ask me about Medicare" button when hosting activities. And during Annual Enrollment Period (AEP) take a few minutes and let them know the upcoming changes.

Rebecca Davis

#34 – Local Services

Hire locally.....

Do you have tasks that need to be completed outside of your business, such as odd jobs, construction jobs, cleaning jobs, car detailing, printing jobs, etc.? A good means to support your community is to hire locally.

Find people that live locally to do the job especially now. Don't go through a big company or hire out of the metroplex if you live out of town. Even if you can do the job yourself, outsource it locally.

I find stuff that needs to be done all the time just so I can make a post and ask for someone's help. It's a conversation starter!

Why....

1. Small businesses and the self-employed are struggling to stay afloat;

2. They know other people in town;

3. Talk about what you do with a simple conversation without trying to sell them your services. Work into the conversation, "Hey, I really could use your help on this because I work doing this and don't have time...;"

4. They will remember you because you might be the person that kept their business running during a slow period; and

5. The bonus, you got the project done.

Pro Tip: Before you hire, do a little background or ask for references/research on the potential person first, so you don't end up in a crazy situation.

Rebecca Davis

#35 – Golf Tournament

Host a Putt-Putt Golf Tournament for Seniors.

Invite seniors to a day of mini-golf. Have your table set up for the participants to register. Introduce yourself and your business. Winners are those with the fewest putts. Give prizes or trophies to the top three winners.

Pro Tip: Ask different carriers and/or neighborhood businesses to be hole sponsors.

#36 – Medicare Carwash

Host a "Medicare Carwash".

Hold a carwash using high school kids who may need community service hours to graduate. The labor is donated.

Each person showing their Medicare card gets a free car wash. Have a table set up with water and snacks that the seniors can get while waiting for their carwash.

Pro Tip: Give away a small goodie bag for the car with air freshener, your business cards and product information.

Rebecca Davis

#37 – Walking Group

Start a Senior Walking Group.

Two or three days a week, have the group meet at the park, the mall, or some other good spot in your town. Map out a path where you can walk with the seniors in the community. This gets them out of the house and meeting others their age.

Pro Tip: As weather permits, always walk on the same days at the same time so there is no confusion.

#38 - YouTube

Start a client facing YouTube channel.

Grass Roots is about connecting with people on a personal level, not just in your immediate area but anywhere you can.

Be fun, be upbeat, and be positive when you talk about the products you represent. Give education about these products and about Medicare. Share Medicare benefit scenarios. Post about what's going on in the world.

Pro Tip: Invite guests from your hometown and from different businesses and give them a chance to shine. These are your referral partners.

Rebecca Davis

#39 – Movie Night

Host a Home Movie night.

Who doesn't like movie night? Go to redbox.com/gifts and order a bunch of promo codes. Give these codes to people on *FaceBook* and *Instagram*. You can also text the codes to your current clients. This is such a small gesture but will get great feedback.

Pro Tip: You may want to use a contest to award the promo codes or put them in your newsletter.

#40 – Podcast

Start A Podcast.

Start a podcast or get booked as a podcast guest. Both are great ways to get your message out.

This gives you a chance to get to know others in your space and also connect with an audience across the nation.

Pro Tip: Podcasts can always be heard again and again, versus a one-time radio show.

Check out these amazing podcasts:
"I Sell Medicare Plans"
"Power Woman In Insurance"
"The Medicare Space"
"Taco Tuesday"
 "Strong LYFE Podcast"

#41 – Hand Sanitizer

Buy a bunch of personal bottles of sanitizers.

Relabel the bottles with your information and branding. Grab an inexpensive basket and put a bunch in several baskets to leave at the banks, doctors' offices, and pawnshops. Get permission to leave the baskets out for their customers to grab one. This promotes good health and your business all at the same time.

Pro Tip: Hand sanitizers may be hard to come by. When you can catch a sale, grab them.

#42 – Partner with P&C Agents

Identify the Property and Casualty agents and agencies in your area.

Reach out to them. Introduce yourself. Invite the agents to lunch or coffee and discuss how you can help each other out!!! Build a referral network with them. Let them know that you don't sell P&C Insurance so their clients are safe with you versus looking somewhere else for insurance.

Pro Tip: Paying a small referral fee once for a reward of a continual payout is worth the investment.

Rebecca Davis

#43 – Food Drive

Host a food drive for the local food pantries.

This is a great way to get your foot in the door to be allowed to set up a table on days when the food pantries are open. When there, you can help sign people up for extra health services that they are eligible for and unaware of.

Pro Tip: Let the local newspaper know when and where you are doing the food drive for increased free publicity.

#44 – Paint Party

Painting with a Twist.

These places have become very popular and are ideal places to hold a paint party. Host a paint party for seniors and invite current clients. Ask each client to bring a friend. Remember no alcohol should be served during your events; otherwise you can create a liability issue for yourself.

Pro Tip: Prearrange the items to choose from or the picture that will be done so that the price stays under $15 per person.

Rebecca Davis

#45 – Custom Music

Use custom music for your phone.

If you have a multi-line phone system or use a landline system where people are placed on hold, use custom music. While they are on hold the person can hear about the types of insurance you offer or more about your company.

Pro Tip: Use music fitting to your branding or to the product you currently market.

#46 – Taxi Billboards

Do You Have A Local Taxi Company?

If so, reach out to them and ask if you can sponsor car magnets with your logo and information on it. Offer to pay them a small monthly fee. In return, you get a mobile billboard. It's a win-win situation.

Pro Tip: Make sure the company is reputable with good reviews. Nobody wants to be associated with a bad business.

Rebecca Davis

#47 – Game Night

Host a Game Night.

Create a relationship with an assisted living or independent living center and host a monthly game night. Pick a game each month that seniors can play as a group, i.e. *Family Feud* or *Trivia*. These games promote mental health and team building skills.

Pro Tip: Set up a carrier table and the carrier to pay for the snacks and prizes.

#48 – Air Fresheners

Customize car air fresheners with your logo and information.

Give the air fresheners to new and existing customers. They are a great reminder of who you are while hanging in the car.

Pro Tip: Order different fragrances, if possible. Remember, some fragrances affect allergies.

Use the Promo code Kannonball15 to save 15%:

Rebecca Davis

#49 – Movie Night

Rent a Movie Theater.

Host a movie event for seniors. Invite current clients and their guests, as well as post an invite at senior housing facilities.

Some senior housing facilities provide transportation and can bring their residents to the movies. RSVP required due to limited seating at theaters.

Pro Tip: Host the movie event as an afternoon matinee. As an added feature, you might give a coupon for popcorn and a drink.

#50 – Tik Tok

Create videos and post to *Tik Tok*.

These videos can be about yourself or educational videos about what you do and how you can help. It's a great way to get current changes out quickly. You can engage a national following, with a personal feel for free.

Pro Tip: *Tik Tok* videos are short. Prepare what you want to say before you start filming. You have literally 60 seconds to get your message across.

Rebecca Davis

#51 – Educating the Incarcerated

Visit your local jails and prisons.

Many people when sentenced end up turning 65 while they are incarcerated, this creates a long- term problem due to them not being able to timely sign up for their Medicare. Upon release, they discover there are penalties for not signing up on time.

As an insurance agent you can reach out to your local facilities where you can offer to sponsor a class to teach them about their Medicare rights and how to appeal these penalties once released.

Pro Tip: Remember to leave your business cards with the facility so they can reach out to you upon their release to help get everything set up.

#52 – Local Grocers

Set up a table at your local grocery store.

Use the local grocer or any other community store where there is high traffic. Have information and branded giveaways on the table. Make sure if you are representing carriers the location, date, time, address is filed with The Center for Medicare and Medicaid Services (CMS) to stay compliant.

Pro Tip: Set up a table every week on the same days and times. I recommend doing it at least 2 days a week, minimum four hours a day.

#53 – Walmart Pharma

Be a presence at the local *Walmart* Pharmacy.

Create a relationship with the *Walmart* store manager and the pharmacy manager. If you are not able to set up a table top in the store, ask if you might leave flyers or tri-folds with your contact information.

Be sure to leave business cards with the pharmacy manager for anyone who has questions about prescription drugs or prescription drug plans.

Pro Tip: Use a small candy jar as an ice breaker with the pharmacy and the store manager.

#54 – A Blog

Start a Blog.

Start a blog that talks about your personal experiences and gives educational content about the work you do. If the blog is linked to your website it will also help your Search Engine Optimization (SEO) ratings and Google rankings.

Pro Tip: It's a great way to increase your brand awareness and position you as the expert within your space.

Rebecca Davis

#55 – Customized Golf Balls

Customize golf balls with your logo.

Use personalized golf balls as giveaways for any and all golf locations that will accept them for golfers' use.

Provide sleeves of customized golf balls to seniors at golf courses. Use these golf balls in gift bags at senior events.

Pro Tip: Many seniors play golf. Find a golf community where you can brand by donating personalized golf balls.

#56 – Easter Egg Hunt

Host an Easter Egg Hunt.

As an inside event or an outside event, use Easter Eggs and other goodies to bring the crowd. Rent the Easter Bunny outfit or hire an Easter Bunny to come for pictures.

Set up tables to display the products you offer and be available to answer any questions.

Pro Tip: This is an opportunity to meet people of all ages in the community.

Rebecca Davis

#57 – Garage Sale

Do a City Wide Garage sale.

Once the location is secured, rent vendor spaces to other organizations for $10 or less and have the proceeds from the rentals go to a local community non-profit organization.

Make sure your booth is set up with the products and your agency branding.

Pro Tip: Since proceeds go to a non-profit organization, advertise this in the local newspapers, radio and television stations. These advertisements may be done as community announcements without costs.

#58 – Corn Hole Tournament

Have a Corn Hole Tournament.

Sponsor this tournament in the city park, at a local sports facility, or the parking lot of your office (if big enough). Make sure to giveaway good prizes.

Pro Tip: Have multiple age groups from kids to seniors. You can even have customized boards made.

Rebecca Davis

#59 – Valentine Brunch

Host a Senior Valentine's Brunch.

Have grandparents bring their grandkids to a special brunch just for them. Keep the food simple but delicious. Have a photo booth and a place where they can make a keepsake together and take it home with them.

Pro Tip: Make sure you wear your "Ask Me About Medicare" button and have a table set up with your company information as the sponsor.

#60 – Ice Cream Social

Cool down those hot summer days.

During hot summer days host, an Ice Cream Social. You can even incorporate a homemade ice cream contest! Have judges do a taste test and give out prizes.

The Ice Cream Social can be held at your local community center, senior center, or with church groups.

Pro Tip: Have a specific theme for the contest.

Rebecca Davis

#61 – Turkey Giveaway

The Great Turkey Giveaway!

Around Thanksgiving, give away a truckload of frozen turkeys to anyone that needs one, right in front of your office.

Have someone dress up as a giant turkey that runs up and down the street to draw attention to your location. Have banners and flags around your location with your branding.

Pro Tip: Order ahead. Get with a store or meat market months in advance to plan so that you have enough turkeys.

#62 - Tech Classes

Host a "how to" class at your office or the local library.

Many seniors are leery of the internet. Teach a class on how to use email, how to use *Facebook*, and how to use a computer. Classes may be once a month or as a quarterly event.

Pro Tip: Ask students from the local colleges and universities to volunteer to conduct the training. Offer one segment at a time and break each topic into three to four sessions.

Rebecca Davis

#63 – Couponing

Hard-core Couponing.

Enlist the services of someone who takes couponing seriously and ask them to join you in teaching seniors how to use couponing to stretch their income.

Pro Tip: People in general always want to save money. Couponing can be profitable for the seniors in stretching their budget dollars and can become an addictive habit as entertainment for them.

#64 – Everyone in the Pool

Do you have a community pool?

Use the community pool or the pool at the senior housing complex to host a Pool Party!

Play music from the seniors' era, provide snacks and drinks poolside from your branded table.

Pro Tip: This is a great way for seniors to make new friends. Remember to wear your "Ask Me About Medicare" buttons or even have a custom swimsuit made!

Rebecca Davis

#65 – Grandparents Day

The first Sunday after Labor Day is Grandparent's Day.

Sponsor a picnic for grandparents and grandkids. Pre-plan games and activities to keep everyone having a good time! You can even make it a potluck where everyone brings one dish.

Pro Tip: Host the event at the local park or a local assisted living facility.

#66 – Casino Night

Seniors seem to love Las Vegas. Have a Casino Night!

Rent the game tables and slot machines. (No cash prizes). Everyone receives the same amount of chips at the beginning. Seniors with the most chips at the end of the night wins.

Make sure you take their picture in front of your banners and congratulate them all over social media.

Disclaimer: No cash or prizes that can be exchanged for cash are awarded.

Pro Tip: Customize chips with your photo and logo.

Rebecca Davis

#67 – Help in HR

Businesses want to be compliant.

Introduce yourself to the business owners in your area. Ask to meet with the decision-maker in Human Resource (HR) or Employee Benefits. Educate them that when employees leave, voluntarily or involuntarily, the individual has 60 days to secure health insurance, and you can help with that.

Pro Tip: Help put a Health Insurance Exit Packet together for HR to leave with the employee.

#68 – Senior Iron Man

Host a Senior Iron Man competition at your local park.

Set up races with walking/bicycling/obstacle courses. Establish different courses for different levels of difficulty so that everyone can participate.

Don't forget to get waivers signed!

Pro Tip: Set up a course for wheelchair participants.

Rebecca Davis

#69 – Christmas Carols

Arrange a Christmas Carol Extravaganza in front of your office.

Everyone meets at your office. Give hot chocolate and snacks. Have a hay wagon set up for everyone to ride through the selected neighborhood singing Christmas carols. Don't forget to include the senior living facilities on the route.

Pro Tip: Decorate the hay wagon with your logos and information and give out goodie bags.

#70 – Grow an Herb Garden

Start herbs in small pots that have been customized with your logo on them.

At the beginning of spring, when the seeds start to sprout, give these herb pots to businesses, senior housing, community centers, and government offices.

Pro Tip: Do this right at the beginning of spring to encourage gardening as a way to reduce stress. Herbs, succulents, and small flowers are best.

Rebecca Davis

#71 – Financial Advisor

Partner with Financial Advisors.

Introduce yourself to the Financial Advisors in your area. Tell them what you do and how you can help their clients.

Many Financial Advisors are dealing with future retirees who may not know the process of Medicare. This is where you can step in and become their ally.

Pro Tip: Invite these professionals to a Medicare 101 event and let them have the floor to tell about their services.

#72 – Disability Attorneys

Become friends with the attorneys in your area who handle disability and injury cases.

Attorneys are great resources. Explain some of the insurance rules that they may not know and become an ally for each other.

Many times attorneys are unaware of all the extra benefits that could apply to their clients once they are approved for disability.

Pro Tip: This is definitely a two-way street. Refer cases to them whenever you can.

Rebecca Davis

#73 – Help Veterans

Veterans need help everywhere.

Speak with your local veteran organizations and get involved by conducting seminars on how they can use all the benefits afforded to them. Great places to reach out to are the local Veterans of Foreign Wars of the United States (VFW) and Disabled American Veterans (DAV).

Pro Tip: Participate in fund-raising events that benefit veterans.

#74 – Christmas Festival

Christmas Parking Lot Festival.

Here comes Santa! Offer pictures with Santa. Set up fire pits and the ingredients for s'more stations. Have a table with crafts for kids to create. Have someone read "Twas the Night Before Christmas."

This is a family activity for all ages. Conduct this event in your office or in the parking lot of your office. Have Christmas music playing and just be in the moment to greet current and future clients.

Pro Tip: Have a giveaway. Everyone who voluntarily completes a lead card has a chance to win a fire pit with all the fixings for 'smores at home. Note: Family activity. Not specific to seniors.

Rebecca Davis

95

#75 - Tailgate Party

Sports Fans? Have a tailgate party.

Host a tailgate party around a big game. Showcase your business by using your customized pop-up tent. Include ice chests with water and sodas. Grill hot dogs and invite everyone at the game over. Introduce yourself, pass out business cards and do a free giveaway.

Pro Tip: Have your logo on everything including the shirts you're wearing.

Rebecca Davis

#76 – Insurance Agents

Be a referral partner with other insurance agents.

Captive agents cannot always fulfill their client's needs. Partnering with another agent to help with their client's needs means referrals for you.

Pro Tip: Paying these licensed agents for their referrals will keep them coming to you. These clients are usually slam dunks and the agent holds the same license you do; they are just trapped into selling one product. This will keep them coming to you.

#77 – Social Influencers

Tap into Social Influencers who are not celebrities but people who love you and are your clients.

Encourage your clients to post on social media about their experience with you or your company. Get influencers to comment on your posts to encourage people to try your services.

Encourage them to recommend you on other people's posts that may be looking for the type of insurance you offer. This is a huge play on social media and works really well to generate free leads!

Pro Tip: Make sure you thank them on their tags and say things like "I love working with you."

Rebecca Davis

#78 – Pie Baking Contest

Host a pie baking contest.

Pick a specific pie and have a contest judged by three people. Award a big prize!

Hold the contest at your office or at a local park. Get the local newspaper involved to get coverage and have the winner featured.

Pro Tip: Have a photo booth area where your logos are prominently displayed.

#79 – Singles Senior Group

Start a Singles Senior Group.

Once a month sponsor a potluck dinner where any single senior may come and make new friends.

Arrange a different fun activity each month and create a theme that everyone can follow. The food, dress and activities are based around the monthly theme.

Pro Tip: Before everything gets into full swing, take center stage in the front of the room introduce yourself and what you do.

Rebecca Davis

#80 – Senior Safety Class

Host a senior safety class.

Go over safety tips while out in the public, at home and on the internet.

The world has changed. Seniors may not be aware of new types of dangers. Get a self-defense trainer involved to show simple moves that may save the senior's life.

Pro Tip: Do research and gather real statistics about the dangers specifically affecting the senior community.

#81 – Needle Point Group

Start a needlepoint group.

Buy several patterns so there are choices when your guests arrive. Offer light snacks. As the needlepoint starts, tell the group about what you do and answer their questions.

Needlepoint is also a great stress reliever and engages the individual's fine motor skills.

Pro Tip: This group can meet weekly and use needlepoint, embroidery, crochet, quilting, or knitting as the craft of their choice.

Rebecca Davis

#82 – Medicare Survival Kit

Prepare a survival Kit for Turning 65 Prospects.
(This tip was inspired by Lavet Ranae Ferchert.)

Put together a package with a pair of reading glasses, a cleaning cloth for eyeglasses, a mask, hand sanitizer, a customized car air freshener, your marketing flyer or a personalized letter, and a crossword puzzle that has your logo or label.

This is a packaged gift that you can customize however you would like. But keep the contents at $5.00, plus $5.00 for shipping for a total of $10.

Pro Tip: Get colored padded envelopes for mailing.

#83 - Free Leads

Do you want free leads?

Of course, you do. Hit up your carrier's Agent Manager and ask if you can do a call blitz. The Manager can arrange to get hundreds of leads from their database that have not been worked or reached.

Schedule a day to meet the Manager. Take the time to sit and call these leads to set appointments.

Pro Tip: This is a great way to fill your calendar without spending a dime.

Rebecca Davis

#84 –Senior Haircut Day

Sponsor a Senior Haircut Day at the local barber.

Partner with a local salon, like *Fantastic Sams* or *Great Clips*, where there are low cost haircuts. Get a carrier to sponsor and pay for the haircuts.

Set up a table at the salon where you can let the customers know what you do and that you are covering their haircut that day.

Pro Tip: Remember to stay under $15 per person. The seniors will thank you for their haircut and this gives you a chance to talk with them.

#85 – Medicare Jeopardy

What is Medicare Jeopardy?

This is a fun way to do a Medicare educational event, especially for a group of seniors that have been to many other seminars during their lifetimes. Make it a game. Have prizes.

This is a fun twist to a standard or traditional Medicare 101.

Pro Tip: Get your prizes from the Dollar Store. (Things like household cleaner, *Lysol* wipes, toilet paper, paper towels, etc.) Seniors love that stuff.

Rebecca Davis

#86 – Senior Calendar

Customize a calendar for the local Senior Center.

Form a group with a local senior center to prepare a calendar using the center's participants. Hire professional hair and makeup artists. Also hire a photographer to take pictures.

Seniors will feel and look beautiful and get great pictures with props for the months on the calendar. Once the calendar is complete, the center can use the calendar as a fundraiser for their activities.

Pro Tip: Make sure you put your information on the calendar. A small ad about your business each month would be great, so that your name and contact information is on the wall all year long!

#87 – Health Fair

Plan a Health Fair with participating providers.

Invite doctors, hospice services, home health care agencies, dentists, optometrists, meals on wheels, senior centers, assisted living centers, nursing homes, urgent care facilities, and any other services you feel will benefit a senior.

Pro Tip: Be certain you have a booth/table for yourself.

Rebecca Davis

#88 – The Mutt Strut

The Mutt Strut.

According to science, pets help seniors live happier and healthier lives. Put on a fun dog show where seniors can show off their four- legged friends.

Have fun contests like the dog with the longest tail, longest ears, tallest dog, smallest dog, and the dog that most looks like their owner. You might also have a toilet paper obstacle course and any other fun activities you think of doing.

Invite outside vendors. Charge a small booth space fee to help pay for the prizes. An entry fee can be a donation of cash or pet food and give the proceeds to *Meals on Wheels*. Did you know *Meals on Wheels* also delivers pet food to low- income seniors, not just food for people?

Pro Tip: Set up a winner's circle where you award the prizes and take the winners' pictures with your logos.

The local newspaper will usually run the story if you reach out to them. Also, post the pictures to your business *Facebook* page to highlight the seniors and your organization.

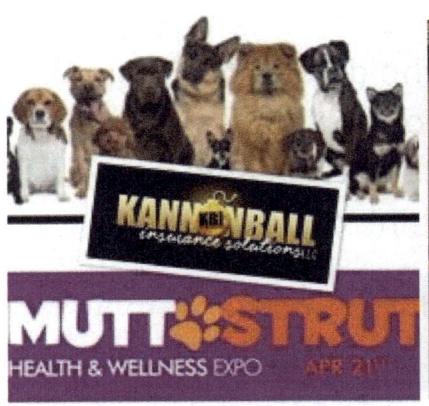

Rebecca Davis

UNITING PETS WITH PEOPLE FOR A LIFETIME OF LOVE AND HAPPINESS
Admission is a bag of dog food or show Medicare card for free entry for up to 5 family members.

KANNONBALL
254-918-5444
Got
Got
Get

#89 – Yard Signs

Order Yard Signs.

Have yard signs made with your name and logo. Add a catchy phrase about being insured through you.

Ask your client if you can put the sign in their front yard. This works like mini billboards all over town. Make sure your telephone number is large enough to read while driving by.

Pro Tip: Print the sign on both sides so it can be seen from either direction.

Rebecca Davis

#90 – Table Tents

Custom table tents.

Have custom table tents made with all your contact information. Then, get local restaurants to display the table tents on every table.

When people are dining, they always read anything that's on the table.

Pro Tip: Have a QR code on the table tent to scan for a chance to win a prize, all while collecting their name, email, phone number, and boom you, have an instant lead.

#91 – Billboards

Does your town have billboards?

If so, get as many as you can afford and get your picture on the billboard along with your business logo and contact information.

People will begin to recognize you around town and you will become a familiar face even before meeting with the person.

Pro Tip: Do a mixture of stagnant and digital billboards.

Also you can get with a local carrier and have them sponsor a billboard with you.

Rebecca Davis

#92 – Kentucky Derby Party

Host a Kentucky Derby Party!!

On race day have a party and watch the Derby on a big screen. Make sure you have a Derby hat challenge and give prizes for the best hats. Don't forget the mint juleps, but for liability reasons, keep them non-alcoholic.

Pro Tip: Give something away to everyone with your logo and phone number on it.

#93 – Outdoor Movie Night

Host a movie night at the park, under the stars.

This is great for seniors, families, and it's COVID-19 friendly. Encourage everyone to bring chairs, blankets, ice chest, etc. Make sure you have a booth set up where you can meet everyone and have them register for a drawing.

Pro Tip: Solicit food trucks and supply portable toilets.

Rebecca Davis

#94 – Dance, Dance, Dance

Who doesn't like to dance?

And, it's great exercise. Start a weekly free class to learn how to dance. Include different dances from square dancing to salsa.

Have seniors come and learn new dance techniques, make new friends, and get their heart rates up.

Pro Tip: Find a dance instructor who is willing to donate their time. Allow them to promote their studio to gain students.

#95 – Bus trip

<u>Rent a big charter bus</u>.

Make plans to have monthly excursions to places like the zoo, museums, casinos, shopping centers, etc. Destinations should be about an hour's drive. That gives you enough time to stand at the front of the bus and do a Medicare 101 presentation.

On the way home pass out a survey form about how they liked the trip. Include a permission to contact section so you can reach out afterwards.

Pro Tip: You're on a bus, so keep your presentation easy to follow and fun!

Rebecca Davis

#96 – Senior Clothes Closet

Start a Senior Closet.

When families lose loved ones, often they have walkers, canes, wheelchairs, and other durable medical equipment that's like new and is no longer need.

Provide a place where these items can be donated and where seniors in need can pick them up.

Pro Tip: This is a great way to fill a need and save a senior the usual 20% co-pay for durable medical equipment.

#97 – A Grief Group

Start a grief group.

Everyone has emotional pain when they lose a loved one. Start a grief group. Establish a location to meet once a week with others who are experiencing grief. Support and friendship are so important when you are hurting.

As a sponsor, promote yourself or your organization and offer advice on how to handle the final medical bills left by the deceased. Assist with any life insurance claims handling or processing. Be a resource in their time of need.

Pro Tip: Find a group leader or pastor with professional knowledge of grief counseling.

Rebecca Davis

#98 – The Senior Choir

The Senior Choir doesn't only sing at church.

Contact the local Senior Center. The choir can be assembled at the Senior Center, a school or church, wherever there is space available. Invite everyone to join and choose a choir leader.

Once the choir is ready, sponsor them to go to other senior locations to perform.

Pro Tip: Have the same color shirts. Make swag bags with your logo and branding. You will be providing much needed senior activities and getting your name out there as well.

9 – Special Occasion

Day or Mother's Day or both, make it a special occasion.

Through your local grocer or florists, order hundreds of roses early. Have little tags made with your name and contact information on them, along with a sweet message.

Go to the places where your target prospect and customer will shop or hang out. Walk around handing out roses and meeting new people.

Pro Tip: Make sure you are super friendly and bubbly when handing out the roses.

Rebecca Davis

#100 – B.I.N.G.O

Do you have a bingo parlor in your area?

If yes, meet with the manager to see if you can sponsor bingo cards or bingo markers.

Customize the cards with your name and contact information printed on them. While they are playing B.I.N.G.O they will see your information. B.I.N.G.O. players go often to play and will stare at your information for hours.

Pro Tip: You don't actually want to have a booth here because they are gambling. Just stick with the customized information.

#101 – Cool Stuff

Do you have a really cool logo or brand?

Create an online store. Add merchandise to your website. Use funny sayings, jokes, graphics, etc. to add to t-shirts, coffee mugs, socks, pens, notepads, etc. Get your brand and your ideas out in the public!!!

Pro Tip: Put a QR code on all your flyers, cards, etc. that takes them to your online store or website.

Rebecca Davis

BONUS TIP

Remind Magazine

<u>Your very own magazine!</u>

With Remind Magazine, you can have a semi-custom magazine made with your information all over it. The company will mail it out to whoever you want.

I like to mail to doctors' offices and T-65 prospects. Using the magazine is a fantastic way to show that you are truly the "go to" person in your area. This magazine also makes a great client retention piece.

Scan the QR CODE below for a great discount on the magazine.

Pro Tip: Be personal in the letter you get to write on the inside cover.

Rebecca Davis

SAMPLE NEWSLETTER

Appendix

KANNONBALL
insurance solutions LLC

Hot summer nights ahead,

    We have had a record-breaking year so far. We want to welcome anyone who is new to the Kannonball family and thank everyone for their support. We could not have been able to keep our doors open without you. We know these times have been challenging for families and businesses alike. As we get our community back on its feet, we are still remaining diligent on the updates for current events as they develop. We do want to express our condolences to everyone who has been personally been affected by the tragedies that have occurred in our nation.

    We know how difficult things have been so we would like to give you a movie night on us. If you give us a call, we can give you a Redbox code for a free movie rental for you and your family to enjoy.

We did get to do a 4th of July giveaway for a Megamaster Grill, it was held on our facebook page and Judy Kennerly won it, congratulations !!

Just a reminder that **Annual Enrollment** for Medicare is **October 15th to December 7th** and Individual Health insurance **Open Enrollment** is from **November 1st to December 15th.** This will get here before you know it, and to ensure we are ready, we are adding some new members to our staff here in the office. So you may hear an unfamiliar voice or see a new face soon. Also we will be reaching out to you in September for any of your life changes, such as income or household, and medical/prescription drug changes that you may have had this year. We did grow our team of field agents. We welcome Isabel in Abilene, Tina in Conroe, Carolyn in Sealy, and Kathy in Dallas!

If you do not have our website information it is www.kbisolutionsllc.com and to like us on Facebook go to kbisolutionstx. If you have problems finding it or accessing it let us know.

Rebecca Davis

Our office phone number is **254-918-5444** and our 24-hour text only line is **254-401-1353**. Our fax number is **844-274-0182**. Don't forget if you ever have any questions or concerns about your policy reach out to us, there is no reason to hesitate, we are here to help!!

For fun we have enclosed a Kannonball word search.....

Best Wishes,

Rebecca

Where to Find Rebecca Davis

Website:

https://www.medicarewonderwoman.com/

Social Media:

https://www.facebook.com/themedicarewonderwoman

https://www.instagram.com/medicarewonderwoman/

https://www.youtube.com/channel/UCy_uDQKvS42xe_S5SxLJfkw

Email:

medicarewonderwoman@gmail.com

Rebecca Davis

Made in the USA
Columbia, SC
07 November 2021